TRANSLATING GOD

HEARING GOD'S VOICE FOR YOURSELF AND THE WORLD AROUND YOU

WORKBOOK

SHAWN BOLZ

Special discounts are available on quantity purchases by corporations, associations, and others. Orders by US trade bookstores and wholesalers. For details, or to contact the author about speaking at your conference or church, contact the author via bolzministries.com.

Editing: Sally Hanan of Inksnatcher | www.inksnatcher.com
Cover Design: Yvonne Parks | www.pearcreative.ca
Interior Design: Renee Evans | www.reneeevansdesign.com

First Edition, 2015
ISBN: 978-1-942306-29-0.
Printed in the United States of America.
Publisher: ICreate Productions, 225 South Chevy Chase Drive, Glendale, CA 91205, www.bolzministries.com

OTHER BOOKS BY SHAWN BOLZ
Translating God
The Throne Room Company
Keys to Heaven's Economy
The Nonreligious Guide to Dating and Being Single
Growing Up with God

CONTENTS

INTRODUCTION

This is a guide on how to put *Translating God* (the book) into practice. Whereas *Translating God* was written to inspire and teach you how to really appreciate the prophetic and follow the way of love, this workbook is written to give you practical ways to make it happen through you.

This workbook will help individuals, small groups, prophetic teams, and/or ministry teams to have new eyes for the growth process needed to move in the prophetic. In it I ask you a lot of questions about how you do what you do so you can make intentional steps toward your prophetic maturity.

Revelation is inspired by intimacy, and as you develop your relationship with God and others, you can grow in your ability to receive and understand revelation and add it to your skill set. Paul would have never encouraged us to passionately pursue the prophetic if it wasn't a gift freely available, one we can develop and nurture throughout our lives (see 1 Corinthians 14:1).

I welcome you to use the following activations, questions, and forms to chart your progress and grow to become the fullness of God's expression of love through his revelation and voice.

SEE THROUGH LOVE'S EYES

"Undoubtedly there are all sorts of languages in the world, yet none of them is without meaning. If then I do not grasp the meaning of what someone is saying, I am a foreigner to the speaker, and the speaker is a foreigner to me. So it is with you. Since you are eager for gifts of the Spirit, try to excel in those that build up the church"

(I Corinthians 14:10-12).

We all know that this life is entirely about love, but how do we receive and share God's affection when pursuing the prophetic gifts? One of the hardest things Christians have to work through is the understanding that love has to become blind. We must push beyond any present negativity we perceive, discern, or have intuition about to arrive at the eternal picture—the one that shows us what God desires and longs to bring about. Sometimes we have to close our eyes to the negative and sometimes we have to look for its direct opposite. We are searching for the revelation of what God wants. Once we see it, we can come into agreement with his higher view, one that overrides the negative perceptions we are experiencing. Once we operate from that higher place, we can help disciple those in front of us into positivity. We need to see people as the beautiful bride, to see them at the end of the race with trophies in hand.

It is easy to relate to people out of your own experiences. You get to give advice because you feel connected to their lives or their own experiences. Your counsel and wisdom can be prophetic, but for the purpose of this workbook, I am going to steer around those and go after the revelatory gifts. Many people will use ministry times to do inner healing, give counsel, advice, etc., but sometimes operating in this way can hinder your growth in the prophetic because you can actually hide behind these things. You're more focused on drawing from your wisdom, knowledge, and experience than on listening for the voice of God.

So many times in our classes people fall back into the spiritual gifts they are used to using, but those are not gifts we're going after (again, counsel, discernment of spirits, inner healing, etc.). I encourage you to hold off on using your old focus while training yourself and developing your spiritual connection to the prophetic gifts. You'll see the most fruitfulness this way. In my experience, defaulting to your comfort zone and already developed skill sets can stunt your pure growth of the higher gifts: to see people as God sees them and prophesy them into their full identity in God.

The same is true with corporate prophetic ministry. Many people will get stuck on what God is not doing, what people are not doing, what the enemy is doing, or start giving advice. I am not demonizing any of these (they can all be helpful), but for the purpose of growth in the prophetic, it is good to spend a season not using any of those tools and focus on what God *is* doing over the corporate groups, what their redemptive purposes are, what is available to them, etc.

Revelation is all about seeing people for their true value. Do you remember the last time you felt fully celebrated and known? That is how a good word of prophecy can feel. It doesn't even have to include a lot of details or words; it just has to come from God's heart. It can mean the world to someone you pray for.

DISCUSSION OR THOUGHT POINTS

When was the last time you felt like someone truly saw the real you and valued you beyond the place you were currently at? Maybe it was a sport's coach, teacher, pastor, minister, or your spouse? Tell the story.

_____

_____

_____

_____

_____

When have you done this with someone? Maybe you inspired a child who was dreaming of what she wanted to be when she grew up, you were teaching and called out gifts in someone, or you were listening as a friend processed a problem and you could see him after the problem was solved. Share this story.

_____

_____

_____

_____

_____

Have you ever experienced a time when you felt like someone side-stepped the purpose of prayer with you and tried to coach, disciple, or do inner healing on you when you were only asking for prayers of encouragement? Talk about what happened and how that felt.

_____

_____

_____

_____

_____

_____

_____

_____

_____

ACTIVATIONS

GIVING A PERSON'S DESCRIPTION

Think of one of your favorite acquaintances. Write down facts you know and love about him (or her). Write down things about his nature and who he is. Write about his skills, talents, and personality. Now read it out loud.

After you write it, answer the following questions:
If someone was hearing this, would he get to know your acquaintance based on your description? If your acquaintance heard you reading it, do you believe he would feel known by the way you translated him on paper?

_____

_____

_____

_____

_____

_____

_____

_____

_____

This is obviously what we are trying to do in the prophetic—give an accurate translation of how God feels about people, either individually or corporately. If someone hears how you prophesy over someone, do you think he would get a glimpse of the person's nature as you prophesy? Would the person you are ministering to feel known by your words?

_____

_____

_____

_____

_____

_____

_____

THE RELATIVE OR FRIEND LETTER

Pick one of your closest relatives or friends. Write a letter to him full of encouragement about who he is. Write about his heart, his love, his relationships, his ambitions, his gifts and talents; whatever flows. Then ask God for a word about him and write that as well. [One good thing about this is that you get to practice being present and aware of all of the best about that person. When you start a prayer assignment for an individual or group, it is great to learn how to begin by focusing on all that is good and right about them.]

Now send it!

After you write it, answer the following questions:
How well do you think you did in encouraging him?

_____

_____

_____

_____

How well do you feel you represented your connection and knowledge of him?

_____

_____

_____

_____

Which ways of encouragement did you find easy to communicate and which ways were hard?

_____

_____

_____

_____

_____

_____

_____

_____

As you thought of him, was it easy to prophesy out of your affection for him or did your knowledge of him get in the way?

_____

_____

_____

_____

_____

_____

_____

_____

TRANSLATING GOD WITH THE LANGUAGE WE USE

"Even in the case of lifeless things that make sounds, such as the pipe or harp, how will anyone know what tune is being played unless there is a distinction in the notes?"

(I Corinthians 14:7).

We need God's heart in our ministry and words, so we need to cultivate that. We pursue revelation to bridge the gap between the things of heaven and the things on earth.

The first part of translating God is in knowing what he wants.

When I pray for someone who is sick, I practice picturing him as God originally designed him to be. I want my faith to have a picture, so I ask God what his original desire for him was. If he has a back injury and can't bend over, I picture him bending over and fully healed, because that is God's original desire. It's the same with prophecy. What is God's original desire for the people you are praying for, and how can you give your faith a picture?

The prophetic ministry can be seen really clearly, in all of its different aspects, in 1 Corinthians. You can look forward to activating all of these in your own life (in some measure).

> *But to each one is given the manifestation of the [Holy] Spirit [the evidence, the spiritual illumination of the Spirit] for good and profit. To one is given in and through the [Holy] Spirit [the power to speak] a message of wisdom, and to another [the power to express] a word of knowledge and understanding according to the same [Holy] Spirit; to another wonder-working faith by the same [Holy] Spirit, to another the extraordinary powers of healing by the one Spirit; to another the working of miracles, to another prophetic insight (the gift of interpreting the divine will and purpose); to another the ability to discern and distinguish between [the utterances of true] spirits [and false ones], to another various kinds of [unknown] tongues, to another the ability to interpret [such] tongues"*
> *(1 Corinthians 12:7-11 AMP).*

LANGUAGE WE USE:

Part of translating God is learning to understand what he is telling us about others and then clearly relating it. This requires conversations and self-awareness—the conscious knowledge of one's own character, feelings, motives, and desires.

Many people have no self-awareness. They have no idea that their words are unclear or that they ramble on with their personal spiritual perspective that only makes sense to themselves. Their words would be so powerful if they could only translate it for the world around them.

Paul tells believers to desire prophecy even more than tongues because while tongues helps an individual connect to the Holy Spirit, prophecy is a love tool to develop people's relational connection to God. "I would like every one of you to speak in tongues, but I would rather have you prophesy. The one who prophesies is greater than the one who speaks in tongues, unless someone interprets, so that the church may be edified" (1 Corinthians 14:5). Much of the modern day prophetic words I hear are more of a spiritual language like tongues than a prophetic language. Groups of people or churches have a common spiritual language that has great significance to them but must be translated to those outside.

For example, did you see an owl over someone? In some circles that could be a bad impression, like an evil spirit in the night, while in other circles it represents the Spirit of God coming in wisdom to the individual. Our job in hearing God is to translate him to the world around us, sometimes even leaving out the pictorial or visionary language translation process. Maybe we are just supposed to see the owl so we can say, "I believe God is going to give you wisdom for all your life decisions." Showing us the picture, as well, might have been God's creative way of getting his heart message into our radar.

When he speaks, it's not just a word;
it's an experience that fully connects our attention and our
heart.

I am the king of pictures, word associations, puns, etc. when operating in the prophetic, but I still have to have an internal conversation with God to decide if I am supposed to directly relate the pictures or if they have an inherent, more important meaning. We only learn this skill set as we take more and more risks and then evaluate the fruit of the risks.

When we do trainings, we find it inevitable that some of the more parabolic prophetic people (especially people who are more seers or visionaries) end up not actually being able to make their figurative language user-friendly to people who don't understand it. I spend time helping them use practical language rather than answer questions with more pictures. This is so important. You don't want people to have to go to your school of the Spirit with you to understand the words you're trying to give them. You were supposed to already be educated in translation (you are in the school of God's Spirit to learn how to interpret his heart for yourself and the world around you).

Most people receive revelations through impressions. It's their number one means of hearing God. You get an image or feeling or connection to the Father's mind or heart. You just know something or get a download of information or feelings. Paul, in a roundabout way, relates to this: "These are the things God has revealed to us by his Spirit. The Spirit searches all things, even the deep things of God. For who knows a person's thoughts except their own spirit within them? In the same way no one knows the thoughts of God except the Spirit of God" (I Corinthians 2:10-11).

We receive deep thoughts and messages from the heart of God that have to be interpreted. We're not just information specialists;

we become connectors of the eternal. We learn who God is and represent that nature, even with our words. This is far superior to just acting as a mail carrier. We are connected to the message.

DISCUSSION OR THOUGHT POINTS

Have you ever received a word from someone else that felt like it had too much wordiness in it, and you wished you could just hear the punch line?

_____

_____

_____

_____

_____

Have you ever used visual imagery when giving a word to describe something that didn't translate well? Tell the story or the feeling you had when you were not connecting.

_____

_____

_____

_____

_____

Have you ever been in a situation in which there was a natural language barrier and you got frustrated?

_____

_____

_____

_____

_____

_____

Out of the following three choices, how do you primarily hear from God?

▷I hear his voice.

▷I see impressions or pictures.

▷I get direct thoughts or hear a voice in my mind (or an audible voice).

ACTIVATIONS

GET FEEDBACK REGARDING HOW RELATABLE YOUR WORDS ARE

For those of you practicing the prophetic, ask three friends how relatable your words are. Ask if they feel you use common language or more spiritual language. Are you giving words using your personal language with God or are you translating it in order to relate God's heart to others clearly? If you do the former, it's okay, it's just time for more growth in your ability to translate God!

TRACK YOUR REVELATORY PRAYER

Break up into pairs. (If you are doing this activation alone, use a journal and pick someone in your life who could use some prophetic prayer.)

Focus on the other person (or pick a person to pray for). Write down all the thoughts, impressions, words you get. Now share what you received during a ministry time with him and try and translate all the thoughts, impressions, and words into one easy-to-understand paragraph. Share that now, or journal it and share it electronically.

_____

_____

_____

FEEDBACK

Get feedback on the word by asking your teammate questions like:

Did it make sense? Were there ways that I could have described or explained something better? Could I have been more concise?

_____

_____

_____

_____

_____

_____

_____

_____

On a scale from 1-10, how profound was it? 1 being a sweet encouragement (which is an A+ for effort) and 10 being something he was deeply moved by.

Remember, your goal is simply to give encouragement. You have no control over his emotional response to it. Focus more on the goals you set: how you deliver the word, how you pick concise language to translate God, and how you stay focused on your teammate.

YOUR PROCESS

Share your process with your team member. Let him hear all the ways you got to that paragraph.

Were there pictures? Did you have any spiritual impressions or feelings that helped you form this prophetic word?

_____

_____

_____

_____

Were there stronger feelings before you reduced them to a paragraph? See if any of these help the word feel more complete or if the paragraph is enough.

QUESTIONS AFTER THE ASSIGNMENT

In reducing the experiential time you had with God in prayer over the person to just one paragraph, do you feel like it left out a lot of detail that would have been helpful or do you feel you were able to meet the same goal?

_____

_____

_____

_____

_____

How much would you have to add back in to make it feel more connected to your original word, to communicate the heart of God behind the words? All of it? Some of it?

_____

_____

_____

_____

_____

_____

_____

_____

LESSON 3

DEVELOP REVELATION USING DISCERNMENT TO GO DEEPER

"You have searched me, Lord, and you know me. You know when I sit and when I rise; you perceive my thoughts from afar. You discern my going out and my lying down; you are familiar with all my ways"

(Psalm 139:1-3).

I n Chapter 6 of *Translating God*, I talk about going past discernment into a deeper place of revelation. Most Christians are fully aware of their discernment and rely on it heavily. Do you ever sense when someone is exaggerating? When you are in a store, can you sense which checkout line is going faster from looking at the people in it? Have you ever felt like someone wanted to escape a conversation despite his poker face? Have you ever discerned someone was struggling with something? Some of this is human intuition, some is people reading, and some is spiritual discernment.

It doesn't take God to see evil, we are acutely aware of it all around us. The whole world can be a minefield that we have to learn how to navigate around, and for that, our Christian discernment is helpful. However, discernment is not our final spiritual goal for revelation. We form opinions about politics, relationships, business, other races, etc. based on our discernment all the time.

Discernment can also be fully spiritual as well, meaning the Holy Spirit allows us to discern something so we can take it before the Father and get his heart on it.

In training thousands of people in the prophetic, I have had the most difficulty empowering them to take a step past discernment into revelation. So many people stop at the inner healing need, the warfare they sense, or the brokenness they get a vision of. These are not supposed to be the subject of your prophetic words. Sometimes they do help build compassion, a sense of empathy, a need for boundaries, and more, but they are not supposed to be the thing you focus on. Only revelation produces prophetic words.

We can grow in discernment based on our life experiences and education. It causes us to be more open to dangers and benefits based on what we have seen God do. Humanity was hardwired to discern everything after eating from the tree of knowledge of good and evil.

Think about it: After the garden everything humans ate, everything they drank, and every cave they took shelter in could kill them. We've had to rely on discernment for basic survival since then; we've had to trust our intuition. This wisdom is not full spirituality though; it oftentimes leads us to just think about surviving or about topics that are good vs. bad instead of thriving and living a full and beautiful heart journey.

Discernment is developed automatically through:

1) psychology or counseling,

2) street smarts,

3) both negative and positive life experiences,

4) experiencing brokenness in relationships,

5) teaching, discipling, or coaching a lot of people.

In other words, the more you experience humanity through different filters, the more you will be in tune with certain tools you use to assess people. My mother has done so much inner healing that she can get a feeling about people's emotional or spiritual health right away while praying for them. She has had some counseling training on how to deal with it, which has formed a different slant on her prayer ministry times at churches or in public. She has had to learn that if she's in prophecy/encouragement mode, she can't rely on her discernment or inner healing gifts as her go-to. If she isn't taking it one step past discernment and hearing the Father's heart, she's not prophesying, she's using discernment to pray through issues with people. Both are valuable, but when we are focusing on how to build revelation, many people will have to fast from using their normal discernment to really press in for revelation.

As a matter of fact, when you are used to moving in discernment to notice certain themes, you may stop there and not even know that God isn't asking you to look at those things. He might be asking you to look past them to see something totally outside your viewpoint.

Discernment is so helpful, but like *Translating God* says, it is a conversation starter, not a destination. I have to learn to use everything I can from discernment but not allow myself to be distracted by it from the deeper message from God's heart.

Picture yourself praying for a young teenage girl and pretend you have teenagers at home. You can probably feel your own teenagers struggle to find identity in purpose and so you may discern that the teenager in front of you has confusion about her purpose and future. What if God doesn't want to talk about that at all, and he is focused on her family dynamics or friendships for this prayer time, not her future or life purpose.

Or picture yourself praying for a single person who wants to be married or people wanting to have a baby. Your compassion moves you because you can discern or feel what is going on in their hearts about these issues, especially if you have personally faced these or know someone who has. Your empathy may outweigh what God wants to talk about. What if those desires are their hearts' hot topics but they are not God's focus for this prayer time with you.

Of course the obvious is true as well—many times our discernment is supposed to lead us—but I wanted to challenge you to think big about your prophetic prayer assignments with people.

DISCUSSION OR THOUGHT POINTS

Have you ever had someone discern something about you and then use it for prayer without helping to resolve anything about the need you had wanted prayer for?

_____

_____

_____

_____

_____

Have you ever noticed when that when you think God is speaking to you about something that you are actually discerning, not receiving revelation?

_____

_____

_____

_____

_____

Have you ever felt judged or judged someone based on your spiritual discernment?

_____

_____

_____

_____

_____

Can you tell the difference between spiritually picking up discernment information and actually hearing from God?

_____

_____

_____

_____

_____

ACTIVATIONS

DISCERN SOMEONE BASED ON INFORMATION

Pair up with someone and set a stopwatch for one minute.

In that time, ask him to tell you a lot of information about one of his closest friends or relatives.

After a minute is up, repeat back to him what he said and add to it anything about the person that you felt about him, based on what you can discern. Maybe it's that he loves animals, is a hard worker, cares about his family more than anything else, has been through a lot, etc.

Now use that discernment to ask God for revelation about what you were told or discerned. Share that now.

DISCERN YOUR PARTNER

Pair up with someone you don't know well and try and pick up anything you can based on your intuition and discernment. These are probably not words of knowledge but feelings you get about him based on being in his presence with God. Here are some simple questions to help you focus:

1) Is he college educated?

2) Is he married?

3) Does he have kids?

4) Has he been saved a short/medium/long time ?

5) Is he from your country?

6) Is he a pet lover?

_____

_____

_____

_____

_____

_____

QUESTIONS AFTER THE ASSIGNMENT

How good was your discernment during the activation?

_____

_____

_____

_____

_____

_____

_____

DEVELOP WORDS OF WISDOM

"To one is given in and through the [Holy] Spirit [the power to speak] a message of wisdom"

(1 Corinthians 12:8 AMP).

Words of wisdom are a revelation of what to do with what is inside of us, or it's revelation to interpret, or it's to give strategy to our spiritual perspective or to other personal prophetic words. Getting words of wisdom is like having a coach or counselor explain what is going on in your heart or about your spiritual or life journey. The word of wisdom is the supernatural revelation, by the Holy Spirit, of divine purpose or counsel from the mind and will of God.

I was sitting with a friend who has probably the most prophecies over his life of anyone I know, but he just couldn't seem to figure out how to activate what had been prophesied. He needed wisdom to pull all of the prophetic words together to create a map.

He asked me for prayer and we asked God for wisdom together. I listened to various prophetic words and we were able to develop an action plan together based on his current circumstances and opportunities. It was so amazing to watch him walk away feeling guided by God to do what God was already talking about for years. Isn't that how revelation is? One communication with God leads to another!

"If any of you lacks wisdom, you should ask God, who gives generously to all without finding fault, and it will be given to you" (James 1: 5 NIV). This is such an awesome revelation gift! It helps you to counsel people in how to thrive by hearing the thoughts of and feeling the heart of God! When people are seeking direction, when we need further perspective, this gift can be implemented and developed. "We do, however, speak a message of wisdom among the mature, but not the wisdom of this age or of the rulers of this age, who are coming to nothing. No, we declare God's wisdom, a mystery that has been hidden and that God destined for our glory before time began" (1 Corinthians 2:6 NIV).

DISCUSSION OR THOUGHT POINTS

Have you ever had a word of wisdom from or for someone? Explain it here.

_____

_____

_____

_____

_____

_____

Have you ever needed or received revelation on what the application of a personal prophetic word was? Tell or write down the story here.

_____

_____

_____

_____

_____

_____

Have there been times when you felt like you counseled people outside your experience or educational level when they came to you with a problem? That was a word of wisdom. Try and recall the experience and what the problem was, then share what you said.

_____

_____

_____

_____

_____

_____

_____

_____

ACTIVATIONS

GO FOR WORDS OF WISDOM

Get into a group of 3-4 people and let someone share a revelation or direction they need more clarity from God on.

Have each person take 2-3 minutes to pray.

Go around the circle and give 2-3 minutes of counsel each about the situation, asking God to process it with the person. For the person who is receiving the counsel and advice, see if you can recognize if there are any words of wisdom or if it just feels like good ol' human encouragement. If you do hear some words of wisdom, make sure to give feedback so that the person who was giving them can recognize the difference between when they were sharing good advice vs. when they were operating in spiritual wisdom.

LESSON 5

DEVELOP PROPHECY

"Follow the way of love and eagerly desire gifts of the Spirit, especially prophecy"

(1 Corinthians 14 NIV).

P rophecy is the ability to know what is available or what is in the heart of God for the future. It is knowing what God wants to do, or knowing what he is developing someone or something to do. Prophecy makes people feel what it might feel like in heaven, as if they have some of the hope that is in eternity now. They can feel like the rest of their lives are important and worthy because they are eternal beings, and they matter to God on the most consequential levels.

Learning how to foretell or share God's future plans with others is so amazing. They end up walking out something in their lives that they feel prepared for, and they get to see God inside of that journey, which causes so much communion with the heart of God—something he delights in.

"We also have the prophetic message as something completely reliable, and you will do well to pay attention to it, as to a light shining in a dark place, until the day dawns and the morning star rises in your hearts" (1 Peter 1: 19). Prophetic foretelling helps you to put faith in God's plan for your life, whether it is referencing a natural provision (I think God has a house for you to move into; are you renting right now?) or a spiritual direction (I believe God is going to open up a promotion at your job as a sign of his love and entrustment to you), or even a relationship (I sense that God is going to bring one of the best friends you have ever had in this next season, so keep your heart really open).

When we concisely learn when we are prophesying and we track these prophetic words, we will grow in so much faith, not just through our own lives, but by watching prophecy come true in others' lives.

God loves to tell his friends what he is doing so they can really feel connected to his love and relationship. Amos 3:7 says, "Surely the Sovereign Lord does nothing without revealing his plan to his servants the prophets." This is a profound sentiment because it reveals his nature. He wants to share the secrets of his plans and our futures with his friends.

Paul regarded prophecy so highly that he sought after bringing prophetic messages to all the churches he visited. He didn't want to come as just a human witness to what God had done, he wanted to see powerful demonstrations of God's prophetic voice on the earth.

"Now, brothers and sisters, if I come to you and speak in tongues, what good will I be to you, unless I bring you some revelation or knowledge or prophecy or word of instruction?" (1 Corinthians 14:6). When you are prophesying to an individual or group, you need to let them know you are giving a directive of something God wants to do and to take note so they will pay attention to its unfolding or until the potential has passed.

DISCUSSION OR THOUGHT POINTS

What is a personal prophecy or someone else's that you have seen come to pass?

_____

_____

_____

_____

_____

_____

_____

What is a specific prophecy you have given that you have seen come about?

_____

_____

_____

_____

_____

_____

_____

Have you ever tracked a prophecy you have given to see if it has happened?

_____

_____

_____

_____

_____

_____

_____

_____

Do you already understand or take mental note of when you are giving a prophecy (vs. when it is a word of knowledge or word of wisdom)?

_____

_____

_____

_____

_____

_____

_____

_____

ACTIVATIONS

PROPHESY TO EACH OTHER

Team up with a group of 2-4 and ask God for a prophecy for one other person about his (or her) future.

FEEDBACK

After you give him a word, ask him if this is something he knew about, has had other prophetic words about, has a desire for, etc. If you said something like, "I feel a move coming!" but he doesn't want to move, evaluate if that came from God. Track it. If it is something he really wanted, then really be present with how you felt when you were prophesying it.

PROPHESY OVER EACH OTHER WITH INFORMATION

With the same group, ask each person one thing he (or she) wants to hear God about in his immediate future. Maybe it's a job situation, a family issue, a ministry direction, a financial or business case, etc. Then pray and write down any prophecy for the future that you see for each individual (or person you are partnered with).

For this activation, you won't know what the fruit will be unless you track it, but if you practice 2-3 times a week and track those words over the next month, you will really grow in understanding your own ability to know what's from God vs. you. Make sure to get feedback.

LESSON 6

DEVELOP WORDS OF KNOWLEDGE

"The Spirit of the Lord will rest on him—the Spirit of wisdom and of understanding, the Spirit of counsel and of might, the Spirit of the knowledge and fear of the Lord— and he will delight in the fear of the Lord. He will not judge by what he sees with his eyes, or decide by what he hears with his ears"

(Isaiah 11:2-3).

A word of knowledge includes supernatural revelation by the Holy Spirit about a person's life. The information is not solely discerned, but includes specific facts that will help bring someone's heart closer to the mind of God. Words of knowledge help people feel known by God so they will believe more deeply in the truth. A word of knowledge usually comes right before a prophecy, healing, or miracle in order to bring faith for its release.

Words of knowledge are a lost art to most people moving in the prophetic gifts, but God wants us to major on taking risks with them because they help people feel fully known and connected to God.

I have noticed that when I get people's birthdates or the birthdate of someone close to them, they feel the God of all the universe really did care enough to plan the day they were born. It gives them a sense that their lives mean something. In the same way, when I receive revelation about a street address, people feel like they are valued by God: He knows where they live. If I say their bank account number, it means he knows what they have and need; he cares about their finances. If I speak a spouse's name, they feel like they married the exact right person and that God is in the relationship. If he reveals their business name, they will love their work more. If I share the college they graduated from, they will appreciate that they were on track for their education. The list goes on.

Words of knowledge help give us a sense that God is in all places in life that are normal and sometimes mundane, but they are important!

Growing in the gift of giving words of knowledge is no more challenging than any of the revelatory gifts, it is just more black and white. You can't say, "I feel like your birthdate is in May" without it being absolutely right or wrong. This keeps many people off the growth track of high faith and high risk.

So how can you practice words of knowledge and take great faith risks? You are going to have to be open to failure. Just like I share in Translating God, I have given words of knowledge that were wrong but still met the goal of loving the person, and I had great fruit in the interaction.

The goal is not information, it is love.

But practically, how do we develop receiving words of knowledge?

1)   WORD ASSOCIATION: Recognize when you see someone and he reminds you of a friend or family member. Ask him questions that relate to this known person, e.g., connect him with a specific name or personality trait you are relating to. Many of the words of knowledge I get come in the form of seeing someone I already know and then finding out how it relates to those I am ministering to. I ask, "Is your name Cindy?" because a person reminds me of my sister, Cindy. Many times it is, but sometimes it might be something about Cindy. "Do you play guitar?" I will ask, because Cindy does, and sure enough, I find out he does too. Once you start to flow in this word association, you begin to grow in translating what you are seeing. I think God does it this way because it causes our heartstrings to be pulled when someone reminds us of someone else we know and love in a divine way.

2)   PUNS: I hate puns. My dad loves them, and apparently its part of my Father in heaven's humor too. I remember getting a picture of a young man in a meeting who was chopping trees all the way to a stump. I said this out loud and everyone laughed, because his last name just so happened to be Stump. Matching impressions you get with a faith expectation that it actually has something to do with the person's real life

is important. Many times we get obscure revelation that is not relatable and we have to interpret it. When you get words of knowledge through pictures, you're getting a direct correlation that the person can't miss, nor can you.

3) DIRECT WORDS: Sometimes these come through thoughts projected from God's spirit to yours, and they feel like they appear in your head. Other times they are just a thought that pops up in your heart or mind. Sometimes you will hear the Lord's voice. I remember one time hearing, "This is my son. He is like Joshua in the Bible," and when I said this, the young man's name was Joshua.

There are many other ways to receive words of knowledge. I don't want to limit you, by any means, to these few, but I wanted to highlight some of the ways that are most common.

When we practice receiving and giving words of knowledge in classes or outreaches, it often feels like we are playing a guessing game until each person hits his stride in knowing the difference between intellectually guessing and hearing God. This is a very individual process. I know many times we will do one of the group activations listed and no one in the whole class will get close for a while until suddenly someone taps into the heart of God and his breakthrough revelation is a catalyst for more. Don't get discouraged on the guessing game. It can take hundreds of attempts before you touch that place that is spiritual, but when you do, you will feel the difference between a mental exercise and a faith expression. If everyone gets way too into performance or they get into their heads, we just reset or do something else and then come back to this gift by doing activations another time.

DISCUSSION OR THOUGHT POINTS

Have you ever received a word of knowledge about someone that was specific? How did it come?

_____

_____

_____

_____

_____

_____

Has someone ever prophesied over you with an accurate word of knowledge? How did it make you feel? What did you think about God at that moment?

_____

_____

_____

_____

_____

_____

_____

Have you ever practiced words of knowledge? What was your experience? Talk about your favorite miss and favorite hit.

_____

_____

_____

_____

_____

_____

_____

_____

Are you a creative processor, intellectual processor, or emotional processor when it comes to revelation? Each one has its own strengths for getting revelation.

_____

_____

_____

_____

_____

_____

_____

_____

ACTIVATIONS

PICK A FRIEND AND HAVE THE GROUP GET WORDS

Get into a group. Pick one person to be the host (who will go first) and one person to be a scribe. The host person picks someone who is not present (whom he knows extremely well) whom you will all be praying for.

Now everyone asks yes or no questions to try to get words of knowledge about the person being prayed for. You can ask, for example: Is the person in his twenties? I feel like he knows Jesus. Is he saved, is he artistic, does he work in a scientific field, does he have two kids?

Everyone in the group can ask yes or no questions. The host answering must be completely black and white, not vague. Once the group has around ten to twenty correct items of information, then the whole group can begin to prophesy about him.

FEEDBACK

After the group prophesies about the non-present person, the host will give feedback on how they did. Example: The person's name is Jim; he is a fifty-year-old black male. His birthday is in March, just like Sam said. He loves Jesus and is part of my home group. He is married, like Janelle thought, and he has two kids, just like Luke said. He isn't a scientist or an engineer like Lauren asked, but actually works as a teacher.* End feedback.

Then the scribe can give the host his notes so the host can determine if they are to intercede for their person or if it is a word they can deliver to him on behalf of the practice team.

PRAY FOR YOUR FRIENDS

Pair up with someone you don't know. Spend up to ten minutes praying for each other and ask God to give you words of knowledge about each other. Write down anything that comes to mind, even if it feels obscure. As you share your list, write notes next to each point showing if it had any significance to your partner. Your list might look like this:

▷ I see a lot of hats (loves to wear hats)

▷ 222? (didn't register)

▷ 4? (has four kids)

▷ Luke Michaels? (That was my friend's name, and the person has a son named Luke.)

▷ Coffee? (his favorite drink)

▷ Hamster? (nothing about hamsters)

_____

_____

_____

_____

_____

FEEDBACK

If you received any words of knowledge, they might have developed or built the person's faith for that subject, so now ask God to speak to you about that subject. Example: In our previous list, the person heard the number four, which ended up being about his children, and Luke is the name of one of his sons. If this was you, you could pray into Luke's life and ask God what he is doing with Luke.

GOD IS SPEAKING ALL AROUND US

"'Am I a God who is near,' declares the LORD, 'and not a God far off? Can a man hide himself in hiding places so I do not see him?' declares the LORD. 'Do I not fill the heavens and the earth?' declares the LORD"

(Jeremiah 23:23-24 NASB).

G od is so invested in his love for humanity that his love can be seen everywhere. Not only that, he is constantly pointing it out to everyone, trying to make the heart-to-heart connection with all of humanity. He is giving us every chance we can have at the life he intended us to have. The presence of God is on the whole earth.

"And one called out to another and said, "Holy, Holy, Holy, is the LORD of hosts, the whole earth is full of his glory" (Isaiah 6:3 NASB). There are so many Scriptures about God's glory covering the earth or covering humanity. This word *glory* refers to his manifest nature. It's not a power, a thing, or just his governmental principles; it is our God! He is so big and has so much love that his love is everywhere.

We know that if he is everywhere, this loving God is constantly trying to speak and connect to humanity. Daniel had no problem with this concept. He knew God was giving a dream to Nebuchadnezzar, who was not a good man.

We somehow have the narcissistic idea in the church that we are the voice of God; that we are the source for people to hear God, and if we don't speak, he will never be heard. God himself is the one who is speaking through creation, people, seasons, industries, Hollywood, and more. Many times he speaks through sources a Christian would have run from (in love).

Can you look back in your life and see times when God was present when you weren't even focused on him or may not have even been saved? That is the beautiful part of God's nature, that on this side of eternity his heart pursues us.

When you are practicing the prophetic, it is essential to treat people as if they are already on their God journey. We have to respect that God has given them a sense of self, a sense of spirituality or truth, and he is in their relationships to some degree. This does not mean anything (or everything) is redeemed, but we can help people see where God's love is already pursuing them.

Our ministry team will oftentimes ask someone, "Have you ever had a recurring dream?" and almost 100 percent of the time there is a yes, so then we interpret it. This makes the person feel way more connected to and known, since it is his dream, not just a random prophetic word he is receiving.

Obviously not all encounters come from God, but when we can see where God is in someone's life, we give the person the opportunity to approach spirituality a lot differently. We get to impart our Christian spiritual culture into his story, which can plant a seed that gets deeply rooted into his spiritual identity.

DISCUSSION OR THOUGHT POINTS

List some of the times in life you recognized God was with you before you knew him or had intimacy with him. Maybe he saved you from a car accident, or maybe you had uncommon wisdom making a decision which you now recognize was his voice and grace.

_____

_____

_____

_____

_____

Has anyone who doesn't believe in Jesus ever shared with you his legitimate spiritual encounters? Did you discount them or possibly see them in a greater context?

_____

_____

_____

_____

_____

_____

Have you ever had an experience with someone while doing outreach (or connected to a person who doesn't believe in Jesus) to interpret something spiritually for them?

_____

_____

_____

_____

_____

_____

ACTIVATIONS

PHONE CALL OUTREACH

Divide into groups of 2-3. By phone, call a non-Christian friend or go visit a stranger and ask him if he has had a recurring dream. After hearing the dream, pick one teammate to tell the dream back in exact detail (this is what I heard you say). Then, as a group, interpret the dream. Ask for the following feedback:

1) Do you feel like you understand why you are having the dream now?

2) Can you tell us what you think the exact message of the dream is now that we have talked?

FEEDBACK

As a group, encourage each other about which language you used individually that was helpful, but also give helpful critique of what could change—one positive and one growth point each. Don't repeat each other's points.

PROPHETIC ACCOUNTABILITY

"The spirits of the prophets are subject to the prophets"
(1 Corinthians 14:32 NASB).

Paul wrote to the Corinthians about this very key prophetic principle. We use the above verse a lot when we expect prophets to be orderly and honoring to the spiritual atmosphere in the room. This verse actually goes much further than that: It speaks of self-managing, being self-aware, and being accountable to the crowd or community they are prophesying to. There is too little spoken on the governing of the prophetic, but that is because the whole Bible gives a relational framework to the gifts—one that prophecy is supposed to adhere to as its core value system.

Paul and the New Testament writers had no desire to separate ministerial roles from the full accountability of the core message of relationship.

There was never a single role in the New Testament—such as missionary, prophet, or pastor—that was talked about more than two or three times. Our main identities, however, as sons and co-inheritors with Jesus, are found as a central thread throughout the New Testament.

It's essential to focus on the majors instead of the minors. When we make our identities the central theme of prophetic ministry or the pursuit of the prophetic, it gives prophecy the same importance as every other gift of God's. It's so important that we keep prophetic ministers, and people who prophesy, accountable for their relational skills, not just their prophetic words.

Self-Accountability: Part of growing is the ability to track change and progress as well as mistakes. Included in this workbook is a tracking sheet you can use as a framework for tracking your prophecies. For the times you are growing in the prophetic, I want to invite you to an accountability process that hopefully will last throughout your pursuit of prophetic gifts. If you are going to grow with intention, you need to be able to measure your growth. That means checking in to see how much your words connected with those you gave words to, how accurate the words were, if your specific prophecies actually happened, if your words of knowledge were on target, and if your words of wisdom were helpful or useful.

Whenever you give a prophetic word, listen to it for which parts were foretelling vs. prophesying. Write down that prophecy in as much detail as you can (example: I see that there will be a great breakthrough in your finances by this summer). You can either do this digitally and set a reminder to e-mail the person around the end of the summer or you can do it manually and remind yourself to e-mail him. Get feedback on his life: Did he have more resources or finances in a visible way? Write the story if he did, and if he didn't, apologize and remind him that you are growing. You are not repenting; you are taking responsibility for setting his expectations and for your maturing process.

For words of knowledge, you can ask the person directly each time instead of telling him or talking to him without giving him a chance to respond. Example: Do you have a brother vs. *I see your brother!* This helps you to get cues to move forward in the word or to stop.

Don't assume you are right or that your information is infallible! As a matter of fact, the more you prophesy, the more you will inevitably have to take responsibility for something you said that didn't come through. This is as normal as a musician missing a note. You just have to take responsibility if you are doing this for someone else.

Taking responsibility for something that didn't work out with your prophetic word should not be a crisis recovery process if you said it in humility. Even the most critical issues can be handled with simple grace. Some people actually create a scene when they are wrong or ultimately pull the attention on themselves, but you are apologizing or taking responsibility for the other person, not for yourself.

You can do this in the simplest way. There should be no shame in your growth process, and if someone wants more than just an apology, he is being codependent to your word and you need to put up a strong boundary. An example of how to take responsibility for something you said that didn't happen: "Thank you so much for the opportunity to pray with you and I am so sorry that what I said didn't happen". Or: "I am growing in hearing God's voice and part of that growth is learning from when I took a risk that didn't pay off. Thank you for being part of my growth process."

DISCUSSION OR THOUGHT POINTS

Share a story of when you took a risk and you were wrong. Did you go back and take responsibility and how did you feel about the process?

_____

_____

_____

_____

_____

_____

Have you ever felt violated by a prophetic word? Pray for each other to release each other from false responsibility for a prophetic word.

_____

_____

_____

_____

_____

_____

_____

Has anyone ever taken responsibility for a word that didn't happen in your life or your friends' lives?

_____

_____

_____

_____

_____

_____

_____

_____

ACTIVATIONS

GIVE WORDS AND THEN USE A TRACKING SHEET

Break up into groups of four and pray for each other with the intention to prophesy. Use the tracking sheet provided if there are any foretelling prophecies.

Fnd the Tracking sheet on the following page.

PROPHETIC FEEDBACK SHEET

Name of person being ministered to: _____

Email: _____

Date: _____

Trackable prophetic points:

Include dates, specific future information, specific names or details of opportunities you prophesied

_____

_____

_____

Date you will contact him or her to track word by: _____

Feedback after you've finished tracking:

Include how accurate on a scale from 1-100 he felt the word was. Was it 60 percent or 100 percent?

_____

_____

_____

_____

_____

_____

WEIGH THE PROPHETIC

"Two or three prophets should speak, and the others should weigh carefully what is said"

(1 Cor 14:29).

P aul talks about how all prophecy should be weighed. What is this "weighing?" One thing I have realized is that we misinterpret a lot of things as a word from God when they are actually emotional responses to circumstances or hormones: God told me I *will* marry you!

Sometimes they come from desperation: God told me I *will* get this job! Then the job doesn't come, but we wanted it so badly that we claimed it by a desperation-based faith. Sometimes it's something we are hoping for: We *will* win the lottery!

Desire-based prophetic words are the hardest because they are oftentimes incorrect and can fill us with discouragement for trying. We can develop a system of weighing words though, even with our ability to hear God for ourselves. If we often exaggerate to ourselves (see those previous examples), then we may have to watch how we share words with others, especially when they tell us their needs.

We have to weigh our personal and corporate prophetic experiences so we can grow. This is often misunderstood, because then people feel obliged to create a tracking structure which becomes just one more responsibility that never gets done. Let me give you some great examples of how you can weigh a prophecy you are giving (or that is given to you):

1) Give/get feedback: Give the prophetic person (who has prophesied to you) feedback. Tell him what connected and what has yet to connect (or may never connect) in your heart or spirit. As a person gets feedback, it starts to grow him. He can begin to feel when a word is 100 percent accurate and or when it isn't. He can sense which parts felt inspired by the Holy Spirit and actually connected with his audience vs. which parts felt like human encouragement or his hopes for good things to happen. He can also then start to learn what is disconnected, uninspired, and doesn't land at all.

2) As a person trying to grow in prophecy, track all information that is weighable and get feedback on it. If you can track what you are saying, write it down with the contact info. Weigh it by watching it happen or not happen.

3) When you give words, record them and listen to them again later to weigh their different parts. When you receive a word, individually or as a community, listen to it again in different seasons of time, and see if you feel differently about it in the future. Sometimes time and space can make us feel differently about things.

4) Get feedback as quickly as possible while the word is fresh. Or if you are receiving the word, give the people who prophesied immediate feedback. Immediate doesn't mean right after, but make sure to share with them what really mattered in the word. If there is something like a word of knowledge that was off, share it with them as well in a positive, constructive way. The more we share what is working with those who are trying, the faster they will grow. The prophetic is a skillset based on relationship, so it will only grow by relational feedback.

5) When you give a corporate word, let it be weighed. Don't try and fit any details in to make it work more. For the leadership receiving a corporate word: Weigh the word based on everything else God is saying to your leadership and community.

As a prophetic person, I am not just trying to see if I was right or wrong, I am also trying to see how right or wrong I was. Sometimes we ask people for feedback and they feel like it meant something but they couldn't define the full meaning for themselves. This shouldn't be a discouragement—you are learning to translate God! It takes a while to be a good translator.

Think about how a first-time natural translator who just started classes is rated on her ability to accurately translate languages. After she is done, her teacher rates her and says, "You were eighty percent accurate in your effort." This doesn't cause her to get discouraged; it helps her grow so she can set a higher goal.

We sometimes are only partially accurate, and it's good to ask relationally safe people you feel like you are connecting to for a percentage of how accurate or helpful the word was for them. This can help people rate us realistically in a kind way.

Learning to weigh the presentation, the heart, the anointing, the communication skill level, etc. can be daunting unless you take a relational approach. This is more of an artistic process at times than a direct science because it involves communication about the heart of God. Weighing will cause you to grow though. Even when I am sharing a prophetic direction with my team, they may ask me, "How accurately do you think you're hearing God on this?" and I am able to articulate, "About 50-60 percent." And we will risk very differently on this as a team than if I say "90-100 percent." In other words, we start to weigh the revelation and communicate that. Then we match it to the history of our other words and take into account the fact that we are still growing in our ability to hear clearly. If we take a risk on a word that I don't have a strong percentage to it and it happens, my percentage goes up. But if it doesn't happen, it helps me weigh it differently.

One of my friends thought he was awesome about prophesying financial breakthrough, but it was only happening a few of the times he prophesied it would. When he started tracking his words, he realized he wasn't as accurate as he'd thought, but he learned how to weigh the difference when he felt something more to his prophetic words than less. He knew he could take a greater risk when he had that spiritual connection than when he didn't.

DISCUSSION OR THOUGHT POINTS

Have you ever weighed your own or someone else's word in a conscious way before? Share about the process.

_____

_____

_____

_____

_____

Have you ever given feedback for a prophetic word? Tell or recollect the story.

_____

_____

_____

_____

_____

_____

_____

Have you ever received feedback for a prophetic word? Share the story.

_____

_____

_____

_____

_____

_____

_____

Have you ever listened to a recording or watched a video of yourself giving prophetic words? How did that feel?

_____

_____

_____

_____

_____

_____

_____

ACTIVATIONS

1) In teams of two, weigh out the last prophetic word you gave or received. On a scale from 1-100 percent, how accurate were you or the word? Which parts were more accurate and which parts don't make sense. Was there anything you could see that was not correct from the get-go?

2) In teams of two, give each other a word and then fill out the feedback form for each other.

3) If you prophesy regularly to a group, church, business, or individual, ask them how accurate and relatable they would rate your words (from 1-100 percent) over the life of your ministry to them. [Remember, you get 100 percent for effort.] As far as what connected or didn't, here is a way you can ask for feedback:

Thank you for letting me pray for you. I was wondering if you can contribute to my growth process in a course I am taking. If you summed up all of the prophetic words I have ever prayed into you with, how accurate or relatable would you rate me on a scale of 1-100 percent? What is an area you appreciate? What is an area you feel I can grow in (I use too many parables, I am too descriptive, I come across as if I know too much, I am too wordy, I don't explain enough, etc.)?

FEEDBACK AFTER FINISHING

How did weighing go?

_____

_____

_____

_____

_____

Can you get a better sense of your accuracy or the potential to weigh your process better?

_____

_____

_____

_____

_____

Can you weigh others with more understanding?

_____

_____

_____

_____

_____

PROPHETIC FEEDBACK FORM

This form is for anyone who participated in receiving ministry from _____ or the _____ prophetic team. It will help us to continue our training and improve our relationship to those we minister to. Be as honest as possible! We want to hear the praise report and learn about areas we need to improve in. If you don't have time to go into detail, please just answer yes or no. Use the back if you need more room.

1) Do you remember the name of the person who ministered to you?

_____

_____

_____

2) What was your overall experience with this prayer appointment?

_____

_____

_____

3) Were there any track able details that are happening in your life right now? If so, can you share?

_____

_____

_____

4) Was there anything said that wasn't encouraging or helpful?

_____

_____

_____

_____

5) How satisfied were you with the ministry you received?

_____

_____

_____

_____

6) Out of 100%, how much did the words relate to you?

_____

7) What could we change about the experience that would make it more helpful?

_____

_____

_____

_____

8) Can we contact you about this form? E-mail/phone number:

_____

_____

_____

Make copies of this form for use in future activations.

LESSON 10

PUTTING IT INTO PRACTICE

"Whatever you have learned or received or heard from me, or seen in me—put it into practice"

(Philippians 4:9).

Remember this: You get to prophesy if you want to! You get to see more fruit than any other generation has ever seen! It is your time!

The prophetic gifts in most circles are expected to just happen. There is still no training room, no practice area, no growth scale. We have to burst this bubble and release an environment in which people can grow.

1) PRACTICING A LOT!

For some reason, many people think prophets should be able to bypass the practice and skill-building process. Could you imagine listening to any mature, well-know speaker when they were first starting out? Out of their first fifty messages, I am sure that several would have been very inspirational, but most of us would have thought, *This person has a lot of growth ahead of them. I am going to listen to someone else instead.* No one would have paid for me to come speak based on my first five years of ministry, but Mike Bickle and the Kansas City prophetic team let me tag along and speak during main sessions anyway. It was their grace, not the host churches, which made a way for me.

In other words, it takes hundreds if not thousands of attempts at public speaking and teaching before you become decent and relatable, and that is if you are doing it in an educated way. For some reason we expect people to prophesy as experts in their first seasons of trial, but it just never happens that way in a context that can be maintained.

2) REWARDING RISK

In our local church and friendship environment, risk should be rewarded, not just success. It takes so much courage and faithfulness to keep trying to prophesy or give words of knowledge. Picture it as being more of an athletic training.

When I was learning how to prophesy, we had an old-fashioned church directory with names, phone numbers, and sometimes addresses. I made it my goal to call seven to fourteen people a week for almost two years so I could pray for them and try and encourage them. We had thousands of members, so I never got through the whole directory, but I learned every day from my time of prayer ministry with them. After a few hundred, I had collected some skill in starting the conversation, ending the prayer, connecting what I was seeing to their hearts, etc. It takes time and practice.

3) CELEBRATING FRUIT

Once you start to track together as a community over someone's individual or corporate words, you get to celebrate his fruit. My close friends have consistently pointed out how much faith I built in them by pursuing huge visions over my life, or by stepping out and prophesying over others. It is so rewarding be around others, long term, and share the testimonies of God's goodness. Part of celebrating fruitful words only happens in the context of committed community. Do you hear correctly and in ways that empower the world around you? Your family and friends will keep those celebrations about your prophecies living on.

4) BUILDING HISTORY WITH A COMMUNITY

"Build history with God and he will build history through you." – Bill Johnson

As you build a history of accurate and connected prophetic words, the world around you begins to listen to you or look to you. People will begin to look to God in you to bring transformation to their issues and lives. Once you start to build a personal history of what is working and you have a measured, trackable list of your words that came to pass, you will begin to grow in long-term influence. Of course, there will always be new people and groups to meet and connect to that won't know or relate to your history, but building it in one sphere helps you to have boldness in others. Seeing God through your history will cause you to be more confident, take greater risks, and believe for more. Hearing God and seeing the fruition of your words is addicting, because you see that these gifts and your relationship to God make a huge difference in the world around you.

David killed a lion and a bear, so spiritually he was ready for Goliath. He knew he had walked out a prophetic journey with those animals, so the Philistines were no match for the power of God working in him.

5) LISTENING TO OTHERS' PROPHETIC JOURNEYS

Go out with friends who have had inspiring journeys and ask them to tell you how God spoke to them and led them. Ask how prophetic words helped direct them and how their own experiences with God's voice defined their life opportunities and experiences. We learn so quickly when we see someone else's journey through his eyes. What God does for one is multipliable to many.

DISCUSSION OR THOUGHT POINTS

Did you ever practice the prophetic? How often and what are/were the parameters?

_____

_____

_____

_____

_____

_____

Share a radical risk that paid off. Share one that didn't work.

_____

_____

_____

_____

_____

_____

Have you ever been celebrated by someone (or a group) for something God did through you? Have you ever celebrated someone for the same?

_____

_____

_____

_____

Do you have a spiritual community you are building a prophetic history with?

_____

_____

_____

_____

Do you look for how prophecies have helped people around you? Do you hear lots of stories about others' prophetic journeys?

_____

_____

_____

_____

_____

_____

ACTIVATIONS

SHARE THE JOURNEY

Sit down in pairs and each share your top 5 personal prophetic experiences that have ever happened to you (in short detail).

_____

_____

_____

_____

CELEBRATE THE PROPHETIC

Choose someone who has prophesied to you and send him a thank-you letter, gift, or phone call to celebrate the impact of his word and the faith or risk it took to pour into you that way.

_____

_____

_____

_____

_____

FEEDBACK

Share how it felt when someone encouraged you about a prophetic word that you have given to them.

_____

_____

_____

_____

_____

_____

_____

When you celebrated someone, how did he (or she) respond? How did it make you feel?

_____

_____

_____

_____

_____

_____

_____

_____

LESSON 11

FAITH = RISK

"And without faith it is impossible to please God, because anyone who comes to him must believe that he exists and that he rewards those who earnestly seek him".

(Hebrew 11:6).

F aith and risk are synonymous, and if you are going to grow, you are going to have to try new things that sometimes are scary or do not make sense.

I remember years ago a friend of mine, a new Christian, heard God say, "Go into that convenience store and stand on your head right now!" She was in a season where she had told God, "For the next thirty days, I will try and do anything I think you are saying to me, no matter how silly." When she heard this she was mortified. She had a split second to decide, because she was passing the store and knew how convenient it would be to just move on, but she pulled in!

When she went in she saw only one employee, but she stood on her head against a wall and waited. Nothing happened. She looked at the employee, who probably judged her to be a crazy, late-night patron, but all of a sudden another employee came out of the back. She looked at my friend standing on her head and fell back against the door. "Oh my God, oh my God, you're real, you're real!" She was crying hysterically.

At this point my friend went over to her and asked her what was happening. The woman told her, "I just told God I was going to kill myself and if he wanted to stop me, he had to prove he was real by sending someone in here to stand on her head!" Obviously they had a great prayer time together and the woman was filled with God's love.

When do you stop risking? When it doesn't pay off at all over and over. I had a friend who used to try and get words of knowledge about people's names. He tried and tried but it never worked. He started to risk in that so much that he actually let his prophetic focus (that he *did* have passion and authority in) fall by the wayside.

There is a balance between trying to risk and being practical enough to do what you are good at. I tell people to risk privately for a season and see what the fruit is. If it doesn't work, I suggest trying again in a year, or sooner if they have grace to try, but trying means doing it dozens or even a hundred times before you give up.

People have asked me, "When did you know you were good at hearing people's names?" First of all, I never feel like I am an expert in getting words of knowledge; it always feels risky. Second, I tried probably close to a thousand times and only got a few right before it started to connect in me, and even then it only connected through a revelation encounter, but I think my faith made room for the encounter. I don't think I would be operating in the prophetic if I hadn't qualified to God that I was willing to be faithful in risking.

Other languages: It occurred to me while I was in South Korea that God knows the Korean language. I asked him to show me things in Korean, and you know what? He did! First he gave me a few city names, that people lived in, as part of a series of words of knowledge for them. This was amazing, but I thought I could have heard those before, so I kept really pressing in.

Then I was sitting with my interpreter in a hospitality room, ready to speak, and I wrote a word in the oriental alphabet, but I didn't know if it was real. I decided to share it with my interpreter just in case, but I was nervous! What if I had just made this up? I showed him my journal and he freaked out. Paul said, "Shawn, that is the name of the guy who is coming today at the last minute to lead worship, because the other worship leader had a family emergency! You wrote his name almost perfectly in Korean." I was like, "Say what?" I couldn't believe I'd written a Korean name. God knows our name no matter our language, and he loves us so deeply.

Another time I was in Vacaville, California. I was in that place of being half-awake, half asleep, and I heard a man's name and a date, and then saw he was married to a Hispanic woman. Then I started to type three lines of Spanish. I don't speak, read, or write Spanish. Being in California my whole life, I barely understand any Spanish words, which shows how illiterate to languages I am.

I was afraid to take the risk, but I asked if there was a Jeff in the meeting associated to a date. There was a man who had that date as a birthday named Jeff. I asked if he was married to a Latina and he was. Then I had someone who reads Spanish come up and read what I had written. It wasn't just a mixture of Spanish words I had heard, it was three coherent sentences. Basically I wrote in tongues and it said: Estoy bendecido por tenar una madre como tu. Eres una madre a todo dar. Como tu no hay nadie.

The interpretation was said to be: "I am so blessed to have a mother like you. You are a totally charged mom, a way cool mom, there is no one like you."

Then I began to prophesy how she was a high-powered woman, but when she got married she had four kids in a row and she had to channel that high-powered business ethic into motherhood. She was learning to embrace that as being just as important, if not more important. I said to her, "You could have been someone in the business world; you have rubbed shoulders with great business leaders. You have met John Maxwell, haven't you?" and she had. Then I said, "All your kids are champions and will accomplish great things, but it takes a champion to raise one. One day your kids will say what I just wrote to you and be so grateful to you." We were all so blown away and felt God's love for her!

The social security number: I was sitting with a couple who came up and asked for prayer after a meeting. I had never met them and they had a beautiful mixed-race marriage. They shared that they were having some problems and asked me to pray to hear from God for them. I heard a number: 525-63-9403 (this is a made up number for the illustration of the story). I didn't want to say it because it was just on the edge of my imagination and could have been revelation but might just have been made up. I could feel God's love for them though, so I took a step. "Does this number mean anything to you?"

"That is my brand new social security number! I just became a citizen of America!" the husband said, blown away. I prophesied, "I know this was probably a very hard process with lots of problems." They both nodded. It had been very difficult to get status. "It's just like the problems you are going through right now. They are hard, but God has your number, meaning if God cares about your citizenship, he cares so much more about your marriage and lives. You are going to make it through this in amazing ways." They felt so loved—even though I didn't solve their problem, they had new hope.

Risk-taking: Be emotionally intelligent and understand your environment, but by all means try new things. God's imagination is huge and will inspire you to do things you would have never thought of. That is one of the purest indicators I have of when it is God—it's something I would have never thought of and it's not just a repeat of the last thing I did. God is so exciting and creative. He uses the prophetic to create images and snapshots of his love that we will re-watch in heaven more often than kids watch reruns of their favorite cartoons.

Think about how Jesus spat into mud and smeared it on someone's eyes by a word of wisdom on how to activate healing. That would be something that would never enter into a normal human's mind, but Jesus, full of the Father's heart, saw this and did it! Jesus is the great example of listening accurately, because he never did any two miracles or gave two messages the same. There was always a new and deeper part of the Father's heart to reveal.

Beware of patterns: I see spiritual boredom come when people look to recreate their success over and over with hearing one thing or doing things a set way. The problem with this is, for example, you might see someone's favorite color is blue one time and interpret that he is going to grow in revelation, but this may not mean the same thing the next time you see the color blue. Maybe it was the color he just painted his room and God wants to show him how much he loves his love for the color blue because it was his father's favorite color—who died but is now in eternity. These are both examples of words I have gotten. If you get stuck in thinking you can do direct interpretation, you might miss the nuances of God's great and extravagant creative love.

We are creatures of habit, but God is a creature of depth, and there is no end to discovery.

Challenge yourself! If things start to get easy for me, I ask God for more and try and take risks that are hard for the stage I'm in. I got so used to hearing people's birthdays that I started to ask God things like, "How about the city they were born in or the hospital name?" God loves this! He wants to reveal way more than we can imagine! He loves when we challenge ourselves to really see into *his* heart about *his* desires! He is the one who wanted to speak to you before you ever wanted to be spoken to.

Ask lots of questions. If you aren't getting revelation, don't just think God isn't talking. He loves to hide himself so that you can come find him. He loves the chase and the intimacy it builds.

If I hear nothing and I am praying, I ask God the following five things:

1) What do you love about this person most right now?

2) What do you want to say about his relationships and/or friendships? What are you doing there?

3) What is he spending his time on? Is it in a job or career or hobby that you love, God?

4) What is his spiritual calling?

5) What are good secrets that would reveal your God nature to him?

Notice I start with the love of God and the person's heart. The old prophetic movement always started with a person's calling, which is really not where the prophetic should usually start.

God is always a connector of heart before purpose.

Sometimes we don't hear because we don't ask what God wants to talk about. We assume we know and so we ask the wrong questions. "How can he serve you, God, and make you happy?" It's a wrong identity question for the prophetic. Our questions should all start with: "What are your favorite things you love about him?"

Go for the gold: Remember to go for the gold! As you do these activations and create new ones, let your goal always be to bring a person way up!

DISCUSSION OR THOUGHT POINTS

What is the greatest risk you took with revelation that paid off? Nothing is too small here. There are varying degrees of experience and even anointing, so don't compare your story; compare your faith and give yourself a chance to grow!

_____

_____

_____

_____

What is an area of revelation you feel would be way too scary to take a risk toward? Like getting a name of a police officer who is walking by? Sending a prophetic word to a public official? Telling your unbelieving relative something prophetic?

_____

_____

_____

_____

Now pray that God gives you the opportunity to do something even greater than this!

ACTIVATIONS

PROPHETIC SCAVENGER HUNT - GROUP ACTIVITY

Sometimes it's good to try and set goals or parameters so you can feel like you are successfully trying to grow. We did these scavenger hunts with groups for years. It's very similar to those in Kevin Dedmon's The Ultimate Treasure Hunt book which I highly recommend. Our mentor either made this up or adapted it for us back when I was young, and it has worked well for us for years, especially for kids and families.

SCAVENGER HUNT

Go to a public place together where there are a lot of people, like a mall, park, event, etc.

Try and do the following ten activations as a group (meaning if you are a group of four, do 2-4 things each until the majority are done).

1) Find someone who looks despondent and try and encourage him about himself in a natural way in the best way you can. If there is an open door, pray for him.

2) Get a word of knowledge about someone's life and try and give it to him. Try and have it be a risky detail like their birthdate or name.

3) Try and get someone's name. Ask a stranger, "Do you know someone with this name?" and if it is his name (or someone he knows), ask God for a word for him.

4) Ask someone if he speaks in tongues or knows anyone who does, and what it means to him.

5) Ask God for a word of encouragement for a mother who has little kids. Be sensitive if they are with her and deliver it fast.

6) Prophetically, look for a creative person and try and prophesy about his next project. It could be someone you observe who is creative or someone you discern is creative.

7) Prophesy over a stranger you would never normally approach. If you are a young, single man, maybe it's an elderly woman. If you are a mom, maybe it's a business man in a suit.

8) Give someone something of yours and then give him a prophetic message about why you are giving the gift so that it is a gift that reveals the love nature of God.

9) Ask someone if he has had a recurring dream and if he has, try and interpret it.

10) Pray for healing for someone who is showing signs he needs it and then ask God for a word about what his life will be like once he is healed.

FEEDBACK

What was the best story that came out of this as a group?

_____

_____

_____

_____

_____

What was the worst story?

_____

_____

_____

_____

_____

What was the highest risk you took? Was this a new type of risk? Did you push yourself in your faith?

_____

_____

_____

_____

_____

_____

_____

What felt natural and what felt like you were manufacturing it?

_____

_____

_____

_____

_____

Were you surprised at anyone's response? Did you get feedback for any of the scavenger hunt challenges?

_____

_____

_____

_____

_____

APPENDIX ONE

DEVELOPING GUIDELINES AND BOUNDARIES

Every community and individual should have defined guidelines or values in how they decide to minister to acquaintances and strangers. The following are our guidelines, given with the hope it will help you define your own or your church's.

MINISTRY TEAM GUIDELINES/PROTOCOL

LOVE: As a ministry team participant, your job is to make people feel loved by both you and God.

A. Love through your words: Think about how you are saying things. Love people in a way you would want to be talked to yourself.

B. Give affection through your words and interactions with them. Be personable. This is not a license to be overly familiar or overly physical in your interactions. Think of them as if they were leaders of the United States—what kind of respect would you give them? What boundaries would you honor?

C. Realize when you are in over your head: Direct them to counseling/deliverance ministry/Sozo when their issues are bigger than a prayer appointment.

THE DO NOTS:

A. Don't be presumptuous: Don't assume you understand their hearts or life stories.

B. Don't compare their circumstances to your own. "I have been through that before. This is what you need to do," or "I went through that once and I can completely relate," are not fair statements to make with strangers. You are assuming too much.

C. Do not prophesy marriage or babies. Some people will grow in their track records and in love and responsibility, so there may be exceptions to this rule from time to time. As a general rule, though, these issues tend to cause more pain than be helpful.

D. Do not give financial or career advice through prophetic words when you have previous knowledge. You can make suggestions, but do not use prophecy in the midst of prayer when giving ideas.

E. Keep the focus on the person that you are ministering to, not yourself.

F. Don't be negative.

G. Don't get stuck. If the person has a high-needs personality, feel free to disengage but be kind.

THE DOS:

A. Let them feel important.

B. Give undivided attention. Don't let your mind or eyes wander to others.

C. Know when to stop or release them. Just give what you have and feel released.

D. Feel free to ask questions about the person and his life, but don't get too personal with strangers or you will make them feel uncomfortable (asking about finances, divorces, mental diagnoses, etc.).

E. Ask for feedback when appropriate.

THE PRACTICALS

A. Record the words for them and for you (most phones can record).

B. Use your tracking sheets, if applicable.

C. Give testimonies to your team leaders if this is a ministry team activity (We love testimonies! We want to celebrate you are what you are accomplishing with Jesus!)

D. Have fun! Ministering to people is about enjoying God working through you and with them! Don't lose sight of the joy!

ABOUT THE AUTHOR

Shawn Bolz is the author of *The Throne Room Company, Keys to Heaven's Economy: An Angelic Visitation from the Minister of Finance,* and *The Nonreligious Guide to Dating and Being Single,* and he is also an international speaker, pastor, and prophet.

Shawn has been a minister since 1993, and these days he is well-known for his strong prophetic gift and fresh biblical perspective. Shawn taught, ministered, mentored, and prophesied at Metro Christian Fellowship with Mike Bickle in the '90s, and in the early 2000s he joined the International House of Prayer in Kansas City. After leaving Kansas City in 2005, he founded and still pastors Expression58 in Los Angeles—a mission base and church focused on training and equipping Christians, encouraging the creative arts, and loving people in the entertainment industry and the poor.

Shawn is a board member and representative of The Justice Group based in Los Angeles, California, with whom he has worked on social justice issues and missions operations around the world. He and his wife are also the founders of Bolz Ministries—created to inspire and empower God's love around the world, and iCreate Productions— formed to produce exceptional media that motivates and transforms culture.

Shawn currently lives in Los Angeles, California, with his wife, Cherie, and their two beautiful daughters.

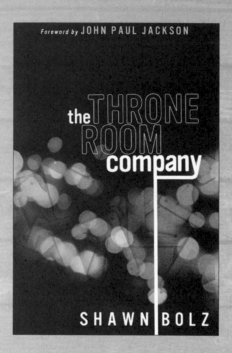

THE THRONE ROOM COMPANY

Thought provoking and profoundly perceptive, *The Throne Room Company* has the power to revolutionize your understanding of God. In this book, Shawn Bolz reveals a fascinating message from Heaven that will penetrate the deep places of your heart. His stories and wisdom will guide you to a more noble place.

This book is about a series of encounters from the author. He shares how much God enjoys you without the need for performance and that your identity is not in what you do but in who you already are to God. He shares about a people who are so in touch with Jesus that they are already living out of the place of Heaven now.

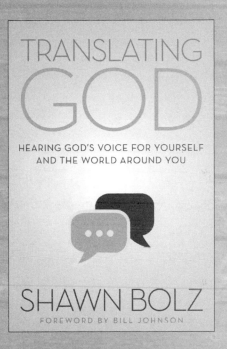

TRANSLATING GOD

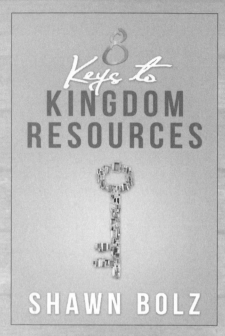

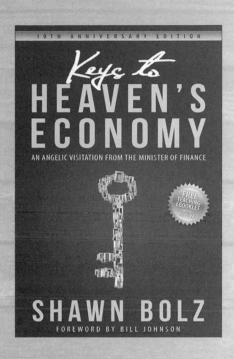

Be healthy and whole

Live an otrageous single life!

Avoid the psychos

Enjoy Dating

Know when to put a ring on it!

Be realistic about your options

SHAWN BOLZ
The Nonreligious Guide to Dating & Being Single

THE NON-RELIGIOUS GUIDE TO DATING AND BEING SINGLE

Find out if you are datable and who else is!

Are you sick of religious advise from people who imagine the worst?

Are you tired of having your freedom violated by legalism?

Would you like to finally hear a few sane words from someone who values love over rules?

Author Shawn Bolz shares from his years of watching others fumble their way through various dating scenarios, but his own stories are the most entertaining of all.

GROWING UP WITH GOD
Chapter Book

Join Lucas and Maria and friends on their everyday adventures in friendship with God!

Lucas knows God talks to him, but he would have never imagined that he would hear such a specific thing about his year . . . and could Maria really have heard God about her destiny? They both have to wonder if God speaks to kids this way. Over the months that follow, God begins to connect them to other kids that grow into friends. Who could have guessed that by the end of the year, their lives would be so exciting!

Award-winning illustrator Lamont Hunt illustrates the rich, vibrant God journey of kids you can relate to. By best-selling author Shawn Bolz.

Growing Up with God is an amazing adventure!

growingupwithgod.com

GROWING UP WITH GOD
Study Course

Equip future generations with the life-changing tools
they need to grow into all God has for them.

**CHAPTER BOOK | WORKBOOK | COLORING BOOK
TEACHER'S GUIDE | 10 DVD SESSIONS**

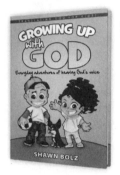  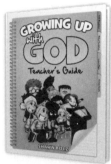 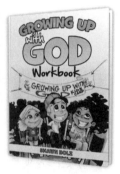

Ideal for use in Sunday school, VBS,
small groups, and homeschool settings.

Parent tips included in each chapter!